# Hsin Hsin Ming
## Inscription on Faith in Purity of Mind

The Tao Through the eyes of
Zen Master Seng-Ts'an
Third Zen Patriarch

A Translation and Commentary
by
Dennis M Waller

Edited by Sherry Thoman

RENOVATIO PUBLISHING

PO BOX 210442

Bedford, TX 76095

renovatio- latin meaning rebirth or to make new again

Disclaimer- The author does not dispense medical advice or prescribe the use of any technique as a form of treatment for physical, emotional, or medical problems without the advice of a physician, either directly or indirectly. The intent of the author is to only provide information of a general nature to help you in your journey for spiritual enlightenment and advancement. The author assumes no responsibility for your actions. Especially if you commit the act of eating peanuts in the presence of Elephants.

www.areyouanindigo.com

ISBN: 1478260599
ISBN-13: 978-1478260592

# DEDICATION

I dedicate this book to my dear friend, Diana Gell. Thank you for your continued support, loyalty, friendship and love. Your passion for life is an inspiration to us all, thank you!

# CONTENTS

# FOREWORD

"The mind is prefect as it is and only false views obscure the mind's inherent perfection."

Hsin Hsin Ming by Seng-Ts'an is a Zen Poem that is often referred to as the poem of nothing. While very short, it is the fusion of Lao Tzu's Taoism and Buddha's Buddhism into what is known as Zen. It is like a waterfall that you listen to. It says nothing but speaks the unknown to those who can hear it. Become like a temple to hear what isn't being said. This is to know the meaning of this poem.

The central message of the Hsin Hsin Ming is to point directly to the mind by giving up judgments and opinions so you can see the Oneness and the Nothingness of what reality really is. The poem professes the need to live life with equanimity, to practice living in a state of non-duality while in this dualistic world. It is a guide to the path of Enlightenment.

It isn't about trying to attain anything, rather it is about losing false views and perceptions. To remove all that the ego so desires to cling to.

The path to enlightenment is the realization that there is nothing to find, nowhere to go, nothing to achieve. There is no need to search for God for God has been within you always. God, itself is your true self, your true being. It is nothing more than waking up from the dream.

# CHAPTER ONE
# HSIN HSIN MING, THE POEM

## TRANSLATED BY DENNIS WALLER

The Great Way is not difficult for those who are indifferent and non-judgmental. Let go of attachment and desire and the Way reveals itself.

Make the slightest judgment and you are as far from the Way as Heaven is to Earth. If you want to experience the truth, then hold no judgments for or against anything.

Attraction and Aversion are afflictions of the mind. When the essence of the Way is not understood, the essential peace of the mind is fleeting.

The Great Way is as vast as the infinite universe. It is perfect and complete. It is your attraction and aversion that blinds you from the Way.

Do not try to catch or hold on to things. Do not be consumed by the abyss. Be still and know the oneness and the illusion fades away.

In striving to attain the tranquility of the Way, the mere act of striving negates your quest. As long as you exist in the illusion of duality you'll never know the Way.

Those who don't live in the Great Way will continue to ebb and flow in the conflict of life. In denying the reality you miss the deeper meaning of reality. In defending the reality you miss the emptiness of reality.

The more your thoughts dwell on it, the further you will be. Still your thoughts and quiet your mind. In the silence of the Way, nothing is withheld from you.

To return to the source is to find meaning. To chase external desire and perversions is to miss the meaning. At the moment of enlightenment, you are beyond external desires and perversions.

Changes that seem to happen in the world are only outward perspectives based on attachment. Search not for the truth in this outward world. Become detached from judgment.

Do not cling to the views of duality. Be careful to avoid the traps of the external world. In choosing one or the other, right or wrong, the mind becomes entangled in dualism.

All dualities are born of the Oneness. Do not cling to any of them, not even this one. When the mind resides in the Oneness there is not one or the other, no right or wrong.

When things are no longer one or the other, right or wrong, they cease to exist. When the mind is no longer one or the other, right or wrong, the mind ceases to exist. When the mind ceases to exist, things cease to exist.

The subject gives rise to the object. When the object ceases, the subject follows. The object cannot exist without the subject. The subject cannot exist without the object.

In the emptiness the two are one and the same. Their origin is the emptiness. Within the emptiness, all is equal with no distinctions.

The Great Way is all encompassing, neither easy nor difficult. Those who live within dualism are wroth with fear and separation. In their haste to be first, they become last.

In seeking you will never attain it. The very act of seeking creates separation. As long as separation exists, attainment cannot be had. Cease to seek and separation vanishes. Let things be as they are and there is neither gain or loss.

When you are in harmony with the Great Way you are free from disturbances. Shackled by your thoughts, you lose the truth and become unbalanced and afflicted.

When you are afflicted your mind is troubled. So why cling to attachments and aversions? If you desire to stay in the Great Way, strive to be free of judgments and opinions.

To accept the world without judgment or opinion is to realize true enlightenment. The wise attach to no judgments or opinions. The foolish concern themselves with the trivial.

There is only one Dharma for all Dharmas are born from the One. Separation comes from attachments of the ignorant. Using the mind to seek the mind is the greatest mistake.

Peace and trouble are born from thoughts. Enlightenment has no thoughts. All division, all dualities come from ignorant thinking and judgments.

Thoughts are like dreams or clouds in the sky. Only the foolish try to grasp them. Abandon all such thoughts of right or wrong; gain or loss.

If the eyes never sleep, dreams will cease. If the mind makes no distinctions, then things are as they are within the essence of the Oneness.

When the deep mystery of the essence of Oneness is understood, you are free of the entanglements of duality. When all things are seen as one, you return to your original nature and remain in harmony with the Great Way.

Contemplate the movement within the stillness and the stillness within the movement. Both movement and stillness disappear. When dualities disappear even Oneness disappears.

The absolute state doesn't adhere to rules or descriptions. The awakened mind at one with the Great Way ceases all doing.

Doubts and separation vanish. The truth is established within you. In an instance you are free from the bondage of duality. You are free from attachments. Attachments no longer cling to you.

All is emptiness; clear and self-illuminating. With no need to endeavor the mind; thinking, feeling, knowing and imagination are of no value.

In this world of non-duality, there is neither self nor other. To become complete is to become whole with the One.

There is no separation in non-duality nor is anything excluded. The enlightened of all ages have known this truth.

The truth is beyond any space or time, an eternity in an instance. Not here or there but everywhere, always within your sight.

Infinitely large or infinitely small, infinity is infinity. No distinctions, no differences, no definitions for infinity has no boundaries. So too is existence and non-existence.

Don't dwell in taking sides or in needless discussions. Reframe from contemplating grasping the ungraspable. One thing and all things move among themselves without need for attention or distinction.

To live within this truth, within this realization; is not to dwell on perfection or non-perfection. To trust the Way is to live without separation. Within this non-duality you are one with the Way.

The Great Way is beyond language, words cannot grasp the Great Way.

# CHAPTER TWO
# ZEN AND BAMBOO

In trying to describe Zen, it is easier to say what it isn't. Zen isn't a religion. A religion is dualistic. Religion has a good god and an evil devil. Within religion there is a choice to make, to either be on the side of good or on the side of evil. Zen doesn't take sides.

Zen isn't a philosophy. Philosophy is a commentary of a particular view on a subject. Philosophy is one-sided derived from judgment. It is man-made, it is the study of issues and problems with an attempt to find answers. Philosophy is very logical, very systematic, very rational. Zen isn't man-made.

Zen is a fusion of Buddhism and Taoism. It is the teachings of Buddha combined with the teachings of Lao Tzu. The roots of Zen are very deep in these two schools. The foundation of Zen is firmly planted on these two schools of thought.

Zen is unaffected by the changing times, whether it is political or otherwise. Zen is timeless. Nothing can change it, it is eternity within itself. It is the one constant in this world. Ever unchanging. It teaches to be in this world but not of this world. You are here so be here in this world.

This might seem a bit of a contradiction. The meaning here is to be in the world and immerse yourself into it, but do not become attached to it. Don't let anything cling to you that will bring pain when it is removed. That doesn't mean not to love or to hole up in a cave. No, it means to have the enlightenment that there is no loss, only change. How can a loved one go anywhere, there is nowhere to go, there is only now.

Being unaffected by things is to be free from the attachment of the illusions of this world. A way to illustrate this illusionary state is through a TV. When you are watching a TV program, say like Brian Greene's "Fabric of the Cosmos," Are you really seeing Brian Greene? The answer is No! In reality what you are seeing is thousands upon thousands of little dots of different colors. Freeze the program on the TV, take a magnifying glass and look at the screen, what will you see? Nothing but thousands of these dots. These dots are not Brian Greene, there are dots! Just dots! Some are red, some are yellow, some are blue and some are black. So, just exactly what are you looking at? A matrix of strategically placed dots to create the illusion of Brian Greene. Nothing more. If you were to blow up the image a 1,000 times, there would be no evidence of anything other than dots. It isn't any different with life. Science has shown that anything taken down to the sub-atomic level shows nothing more than mostly empty space, like the image on the TV screen, there really isn't anything there.

On attachment, treat life the way you watch a movie. When you go to the movies, you suspend your logic and sense of belief for those few hours. During the movie, you laugh, you cry, you feel and connect to the characters and their lives there on the screen. However, once the movie is finished, you get up and leave the theater. You leave the experience behind. You do not run up to the screen and try to peel the character off the screen so you may possess it and take it home nor do you grieve for the movie ending. It's just a movie. You know that whenever you want to experience those feelings, you simply watch the movie again.

It is the same with this life. Immerse yourself into life and enjoy it to the fullest, after all, that is why you are here. Become rooted and grounded into this world. But remember not to let attachments, judgments, or opinions cloud your nature. Be unchanging in your inner true self, your Buddha-nature. Yielding but unchanging. Live in the now for that is where eternity resides.

Overcome duality to discover your Buddha-nature. See past the obstacles of movement and rest. Be of one mind. One-mind is considered in a meditative context to be free of duality. When the mind is free from things and free from attachments, it can function in this world and still be uninfluenced by the actions of the world. Once the attachments have been removed, the true substance can be revealed to you. To live in this faith is to be free from duality while living in a dualistic world.

To live a true life, is to have no need to make waves on the ocean when there is no wind. For this is the way of a Zen

Master.

So, what does this have to do with Bamboo? Bamboo is considered a symbol of Zen. It is a tree that has great roots firmly planted into the soil. Strength comes from its strong roots. It is this strength of being so grounded into the soil that allows it to be yielding when confronted with adversarial winds and storms.

It is always green, in winter, spring, summer or fall, always green, always full of life, always growing, always unchanging. Bamboo is empty inside, clinging to nothing in this world other than the substance needed to support its life. It's soul isn't cluttered with senseless desires or opinions. It remains empty, one with the nothingness. Yes, bamboo makes for an excellent symbol for Zen.

# CHAPTER THREE
# A BRIEF HISTORY OF THE FIRST
# PATRIARCHS

Seng-Ts'an {?-606} There is very little information concerning the life of Chien-chih Seng-Ts'an, {in Japanese, Kanchi Sosan} also known as Jianzhi Sengcan. Sengcan, {meaning "Gem Monk"} was the name given to him by Huike. What is known about him is he was the Third Patriarch of Ch'an, {in Japanese, Zen} a school of Mayayana Buddhism. His death is reported to be in the year 606.

Since we have so little information on Seng-Ts'an, lets look at the history leading up to Seng-Ts'an to get a better idea of who he was. By seeing who preceded Seng-Ts'an, we can get a clearer picture into the type of person he was and of the life he lived. What is really interesting are the similarities between these patriarchs. Notice how Seng-Ts'an, Huike and Daoxin all had similar first encounters as well as their first moment of enlightenment.

The first Patriarch was Bodhidharma who lived during the 5th and 6th century. Bodhidharma is credited with the beginning of Ch'an Tsung, or the inner light school of Buddhist in China. He also, according to legend, brought martial arts to the Shaolin school which later served as the foundation of Shaolinquan. He instilled in these Shaolin schools a collection of martial arts to be taught. It is through mastering these martial arts that allowed a monk to become a master in a physical and spiritual sense. The reason Bodhidharma brought these teachings to the Shaolin Monastery because he was dismayed at the pitiful physical condition of the Shaolin Monks at the time of his visit.

There are several legends surrounding Bodhidharma. Many of which are still recited and used today throughout Zen traditions worldwide. One such legend is the one when Bodhidharma went to Nanking around 520. This story shows the power and respect that he had among the common man and Emperors alike. Upon arriving in Nanking, the Emperor desired to meet him. There was a great out pouring of people and monks from far and wide who wanted to get a glimpse of this great master. The royal court was brought to session to honor the presence of Bodhidharma in Nanking. At this ceremony, the Emperor told Bodhidharma of all his good works, of building monasteries, supporting the translation of spiritual text and all of his charitable deeds throughout the lands. When the Emperor was finished with his inventory of his good works, he asked Bodhidharma how much merit he had obtained. Now consider that this is a reasonable question to ask when one understands the principles of Mahayana doctrine. One of the principles is taking a gradualist approach to enlightenment through your actions. This practice is wildly acceptable within this doctrine. However Bodhidharma replied, "No merit whatsoever!" This surprised and shocked the Emperor.

The Emperor thought for awhile and came back with this question, "What is the first principle of Buddhism?" A logical question so the Emperor thought. Bodhidharma replied, "There isn't one, since all is emptiness, nothing can be called holy." After hearing this complex statement the Emperor asked, "Then who are you?" Bodhidharma replied, "I don't know" then proceeded to leave Nanking.

The point Bodhidharma was making to the Emperor was that he, Bodhidharma was a living example of meaninglessness. Therefore do not ask me what the meaning is because there is no meaning. Bodhidharma said that one should be meaningless like a flower or to be meaningless like a cloud. Being in a state of meaninglessness, there is no evil, therefore no need for good.

It is said that after leaving Nanking, Bodhidharma went northwards and settled into a cave and stared at the cave wall for 9 years in complete silence. Afterwards, this is when Bodhidharma went to the Shaolin Monastery to teach them in the way of the Eighteen Arhat Hands, which consisted of combat skills and techniques.

The second Patriarch was Dazu Huike {487-593} and like Bodhidharma and Seng-Ts'an, little is really known about him. However there are legends about Dazu Huike, according to one, Dazu Huike was a noted scholar in Buddhist scriptures, classical Chinese text and versed in Taoism. While he was considered to be an authority on these subjects he wasn't well received by many because of his lack of spiritual training under a master. This is where it gets interesting. In 528, Dazu Huike was about 40 years old when he approached Bodhidharma. At first Bodhidharma turned him away and refused to teach him saying that he was unworthy as a student. Bodhidharma remarks to Dazu Huike were, "Why would you seek the truth when you have so little wisdom and virtue? With such a shallow heart and an arrogant mind, it would be a waste of time to teach you."

Standing in front of Bodhidharma's cave all night during a heavy snowfall found Dazu Huike in the morning with snow up to his waist. Upon seeing Huike in the morning, Bodhidharma asked him why he was there. Huike replied that he wanted a teacher to open the gates of universal compassion to liberate beings. At this point, Huike cut off his left arm and presented it to Bodhidharma as a token of his sincerity.

With this demonstration Bodhidharma accepted him as a student and gave him the name, Huike, which means wisdom and capacity. Prior to that fateful morning, Huike's name had been Shenguang. Huike ended up studying with Bodhidharma for about 6 years.

Another interesting story about Huike is referred to as the "Pacifying the mind." Huike said to Bodhidharma, "My mind is anxious. Please pacify it." Bodhidharma replied, "Bring me your mind and I'll pacify it." Huike said, "Although I've sought it, I cannot find it." Bodhidharma replied, "There! I have pacified your mind."

14

The story attributed to the awakening of Huike is when Bodhidharma and him were climbing up "Few Houses Peak." When Bodhidharma asked Huike where they were going, Huike replied, "Please go right ahead-that's it." Bodhidharma retorted, "If you go right ahead, you cannot move a step." Upon hearing these words, it is said that Huike became enlightened.

The legend concerning the transmission of knowledge and wisdom to Huike making him the second patriarch is when Bodhidharma desired to leave China and return to India. Prior to his departure, he gave a test to his students, gathering them together, he asked the following question, "Can each of you say something to demonstrate your understanding?" Dao Fu stood up and said, "It is not bound by words or phrases, nor is it separate from words and phrases. This is the function of the Tao" Bodhidharma's reply was, "You have attained my skin." The Nun, Zong Chi was next and said, "It is like a glorious glimpse of the realm of Akshobya Buddha, seen once, it need not be seen again." Bodhidharma replied, "You have my flesh." Dao Yu then said, "The four elements are all empty. The five skandhas are without actual existence. Not a single dharma can be grasped." Bodhidharma replied, "You have attained my bones." Lastly, Huike came forwarded, bowed deeply in silence, then stood up without saying a word. At this Bodhidharma said, "You have attained my marrow." With this Bodhidharma passed the ceremonial robe and beggar's bowl of dharma succession to Huike thus making him the second patriarch.

Bodhidharma disappeared, either returning to India or he died along the way.

This brings us to Seng-Ts'an. Seng-Ts'an was in his forties too when he desired to attain enlightenment. Like Huike, Seng-Ts'an spent about 6 years studying with his master. There is a story of their meeting that is interesting and similar to Huike's meeting with Bodhidharma. Upon meeting Huike, it is said that Seng-Ts'an had leprosy. Huike dismissed him by saying, "You have leprosy, what could you want from me?" Seng-Ts'an replied, "Even if my body is sick, the heart and mind of a sick person is no different than that of a well person." This so impressed Huike that he took on Seng-Ts'an as a student.

Another compelling story about Huike and Seng-Ts'an is when Seng-Ts'an asked Huike to purify him of his sins. Huike told Seng-Ts'an to bring him his sins and he would purify him. Contemplating the request for a moment, Seng-Ts'an replied, "I have searched for my sins but I cannot find them." Huike reply was, "Then I have purified you." Upon hearing these words, it is said that Seng-Ts'an's awareness blossomed into enlightenment.

Huike knew early on that Seng-Ts'an would be his successor. During the 570's when Huike passed on to Seng-Ts'an the transmission of knowledge and wisdom of dharma succession thus making him the third patriarch, he warned Seng-Ts'an to hide in the mountains to escape the persecution of the Buddhist Monks that was taking place throughout the lands. It is said that Seng-Ts'an hid first at

Wangong mountain in Yixian, then on to Sikong mountain in southwestern Anhui. He spent over 10 years wandering throughout the lands calling no place home to avoid persecution and capture. Once the political climate was restored and Buddhism returned to its previous state, Seng-Ts'an renewed his teachings.

He met Daoxin in 592 and taught him the way for 9 years. Daoxin became the successor to Seng-Ts'an making him the forth patriarch. Daoxin was only 14 years old when he met Seng-Ts'an. At their first encounter, Daoxin asked Seng-Ts'an, "I asked for the Masters compassion. Please instruct me on how to achieve release." Seng-Ts'an asked him, "Who is constraining you." Daoxin replied, "There is no such person." Seng-Ts'an replied, "Then why seek such release if no one is constraining you?" It is upon hearing these words from Seng-Ts'an that Daoxin attained enlightenment.

When the transmission to Daoxin was complete, Seng-Ts'an returned to Wangong mountain. It is here where he died in 606 under a tree during a Dharma assembly.

Seng-Ts'an is best known for his poem, Hsin Hsin Ming, or Inscription of Faith on Mind. While a short poem of less than a thousand words, it is as profound as Lao Tzu's Tao Te Ching. Seng-ts'an's poem is an excellent example of Taoism through the eyes of a Zen Master.

The central theme of the Hsin Hsin Ming is to bring attention to the mind in giving up the duality of one-sided views so you can see the "One Suchness" of reality as it really is. The poem stresses the need to take all experience, good or bad, with a sense of equanimity. The Hsin Hsin Ming deals directly with attaining a state of non-duality through practice and mediation. Using the principles of his poem, one can break free from the constricted nature of living in a dualistic world.

This is where the Hsin Hsin Ming and the Tao Te Ching are very similar. This also serves as evidence of Lao Tzu's work surviving and thriving over a thousand years later. It is interesting to see Lao Tzu's work from the perspective of a Zen Master. None of the core beliefs are missing, only enhanced. Seng-Ts'an's poem definitely complements the work of Lao Tzu.

# CHAPTER FOUR
# ENLIGHTENMENT

All enlightenment is sudden. The real question is how long does it take to get there. On these instances of sudden enlightenment, it usually happens in a moment of crystal clarity. These moments are also called having an epiphany. All of us have had at one time or another one of these moments of a major break-through. Some of us call it a light bulb moment when the light comes on when we have that "ah, now I get it" moment. If you were to recall one of those moments, you'll see that you were more than likely in a state of deep contemplation. It is when you are in these intense deep states of contemplation that profound answers are reveled to you. It doesn't matter if it is a math problem or trying to solve a serious issue within your life, the answers always seem to appear during these states of intense deep contemplation.

A way to explain sudden enlightenment is to imagine yourself in a dark room groping for the light switch. Some people find the light switch rather quickly while others spend countless hours in search of the light switch. And there are those who are content to just sit in the middle of the room and do nothing. This is true of searching for enlightenment. It is through contemplation that one finds the answers.

Imagine that contemplation is the process of doubt. The

doubt being that it doesn't have to be this way and no other. It is the doubt that drives you to find that other way. The greater the doubt, the greater the resolve in finding what it is that you are looking for. The lesser the doubt, the lesser the commitment will be and if there is no doubt, then no movement or desire to look.

If you doubt or refuse to accept the darkness, and have great desire, as great as your doubt that things do not have to stay this way, you're going to do something about it and start looking for that switch. No matter how intense your resolve is to find the switch, once found and turned on, the light appears in an instance.

However, if you are content with the darkness and accept it, then there is no doubt in your life, because you accept it. Therefore, you have no desire or motivation to do anything about it. You will continue to sit there in the dark till the end of time. Even worse, is if you take no action because you believe that there is no other way of living besides living in the dark. Either way, you are confined to the darkness until you have a change of state within your mind. You are stuck because you do not doubt the situation nor do you contemplate on how to change it.

Within Ch'an and Zen, contemplation is the art of taking dead words and bringing life to them. It is through contemplation that you begin to place yourself into the question and strive to understand what it is that you are to learn. This is where doubt plays a major role. By doubting that you think you understand, you look for other answers and meanings. At first the statement or question seems to be confusing. For example, the gong'an, " One day a monk asked Master Zhaozhou, "Does a dog have Buddha-nature or not." Zhaozhou replied," No!"

It is known in Buddhist teachings that all sentient beings have Buddha-nature, even dogs. So what is the point that Zhaozhou is making here? From the onset you know this statement makes no sense. You doubt that Zhaozhou meant for us to take this statement at face value, you know there has to be more to it but what? Through contemplation, creating doubt and questioning, you are able to break through the doubt and reach oneness. It is in this state of no-mind where there is no-self that the statement makes sense. This process is done without thinking as much as it is done through immersion by reflection. Even Rene Descartes said, "If you would be a seeker after the truth, it is necessary that at least once in your life you doubt, as far as possible; all things. Break free and live life on your own terms. Think for yourself."

It is with the practice of great doubt in contemplation that you see the real question that the monk asked. In reality, by the monk asking the question, it demonstrated that he, the monk, did not have presence of Buddha-nature. In reality, the monk was asking if he had Buddha-nature. If he had awareness of his own Buddha-nature, he wouldn't have asked the question. Therefore, the answer was "No!" You have got to believe it before you can know it and if you don't believe it, then it isn't so.

Like being in that dark room, if you do not believe that there is a light switch that can illuminate the room for you, then there is no light switch in your reality. So why would you ask if there is a light switch in the other room for someone else? This is the point to the answer.

If you are in that dark room and refuse to believe that there is nothing more than the darkness, then you have created doubt. When you create doubt, you must believe that there must be more to what you see. With this doubt, you enter into a state of contemplation. It is this state that drives you to feel along the walls for that switch, searching for an answer, even if you are unsure just exactly what that answer is. On finding the switch, illumination comes in an instance, it doesn't matter how long the journey might have been to get to that point, enlightenment comes in an instance. In that instance, all within the room is revealed to you and in addition, the door from which to leave!

The key to enlightenment then is contemplation. It is a universal concept, whether it is Jewish or Christian Mysticism, Eastern or Western faiths. Contemplation is a central point in all spiritual traditions. In the west it might be called prayer, in the east it is referred to as mediation, whatever you want to call it, it is the primary path to enlightenment.

So, what does life look like when someone has attained enlightenment. According to an old Buddhism proverb, "The unenlightened chop wood and carry water. When one becomes enlightened, he chops wood and carries water." I have been asked several times what this means as it makes no sense to most people in the beginning. Most people believe that upon enlightenment something mysterious happens and you attain some special power. Well, in a way you do, but not in the way most people think. The power is in the heightened state of awareness that you have. It is in the ability to see what is in front of you that others cannot see. I want to answer the question with this quote about something as simple as building a fire in the fireplace at home during the winter to keep warm. You'll see what I mean by having awareness attained through enlightenment. This quote sums it up rather well, let me know what you think,

"Upon returning home on a cold winter night, I begin my evening by building a fire in the fireplace to chase away the chill. Once I have gathered the logs and placed them so, I start the fire. At the birth of the flames starting to flicker among the logs, it is in that moment I know that I am releasing all the memories that have been stored up in that tree. I know that I am releasing the sunshine that gave warmth to that tree , that tree from whence the firewood came. I know that I am releasing the clouds that gave it shade, the rain that quenched its thirst, the soil from which it received its nourishment, and all those enjoyments that the tree experienced so joyfully, like those memories of the autumn breeze caressing its leaves and the still of the moonlight on a winter night while that tree stood stoic in deep contemplation. And in the knowing of giving shelter in the spring and being a refuge to the song birds and the animals that called it home. Yes, while I witness the flickering of those flames, I see all of this and more, for the log in the fire is more than what it seems. It is at once an explosion of all its life's experiences and joys, and a reminder of what we leave behind, for this log has shown me, how even I, am connected to it all."

Enlightenment and awareness for the most part are one and the same, you cannot have enlightenment without having a heightened sense of awareness. Like in the quote above, there is a profound sense of inner-connectiveness through awareness that everything that is here is all part of something greater, that there is a Oneness, a one-mind and we are part of it. This is enlightenment.

The western world believes that with enlightenment, you attain some magical insight into the universe, that you receive some great dose of wisdom and knowledge. The truth is, enlightenment isn't about gaining. It is about losing. Enlightenment is the realization of the truth that there is nothing to find or attain. That truth becomes revealed in dropping all attachments, and all desires. In enlightenment, you see that there is nothing to know, that by losing it all, there is no need to attain anything. Enlightenment is the freedom from attachments and the need to be attached to anything or anybody.

# CHAPTER FIVE
# ON MEANING AND NOTHINGNESS

Throughout Buddhism, Taoism and Zen there it much talk and mention about Nothingness, Emptiness, Oneness, the Void, and Suchness. In the western world, this makes no sense, "There has to be something, even nothing is something, right?" The western world cannot understand these meanings, maybe because there are no meaning to these words in the East. This is a major conflict between the two worlds. The west always believes that there is meaning in everything, there is always a "why" and a meaning to that "why." In Zen, in the true meaning of life, there is no meaning. In Zen, it is call existence. In existence, there is no need for a meaning or explanation, it just is what it is.

There is a story about Picasso the painter. One day an observer watched Picasso start a painting. As the day wore on Picasso continued to paint till he finished with the work in the afternoon. Upon completion, the observer asked Picasso what the painting represented, what was the meaning of it. Picasso became upset, angry, even mad. He shouted, "Go ask the roses in the garden what is the meaning of the roses! Why do people come to me and ask for the meaning? If the rose can be there without any meaning, then why can't my painting be there without any meaning?"

Meanings are a thing of the mind. It is the mind that seeks a meaning to everything. Sometimes this is a good thing, like in science and medicine. But for nature, there is no meaning, there is only just is. This is the precept of existence in nature, for there is no need for meaning. Look at it this way, how absurd would it be to ask a cloud, "What is the meaning of this? Why are you here and where did you come from?" I am sure the cloud will have no answer for you. Because the cloud is being a cloud, doing what clouds do. That is the dharma of a cloud and it is fulfilling that dharma. It would be the same thing if you asked a dog why it barks. What do you think the answer would be? The dog cannot answer the question, because it doesn't understand why you're asking such a question. Dogs bark and cats meow, because that is their nature.

If a sentient being is living its dharma, there is no need for meaning, its existence is enough. All throughout nature, there isn't any meaning placed on anything by nature. It is us that has a ego driven need for meaning and to place meaning on things. If we do not have meaning we began to feel insecure and worried. We feel out of place or disconnected. This behavior isn't seen in nature, only in man.

In creating meaning, we create separation. As long as we are in separation, there can be no enlightenment. Enlightenment is losing separation and meaning. When you focus on the meaning of something, you have missed the point, because the something really isn't what it appears to be.

On the subject of Nothingness being the primary objective of Zen. Brian Greene, the noted Physicist from Colombia University wrote a great book called, "The Fabric of the Cosmos." The book has also been made into a TV series shown on PBS. In his book, there is a section on, "What is Space." This is where I will show you that science is catching up to Eastern Thought on nothingness. To quote Brian Greene from the show on "What is Space,"

"We think of our world as filled with stuff, like buildings and cars, buses and people. And nowhere does that seem more apparent than in a crowded city like New York.

Yet all around the stuff that makes up our everyday world is something just as important but far more mysterious: the space in which all this stuff exists.

To get a feel for what I'm talking about, let's stop for a moment and imagine. What if you took all this stuff away? I mean all of it: the people, the cars and buildings. And not just the stuff here on Earth, but the earth itself; what if you took away all the planets, stars and galaxies? And not just the big stuff, but tiny things down to the very last atoms of gas and dust; what if you took it all away? What would be left?

Most of us would say "nothing." And we'd be right. But strangely, we'd also be wrong. What's left is empty space. And as it turns out, empty space is not nothing. It's something, something with hidden characteristics as real as all the stuff in our everyday lives.

In fact, space is so real it can bend, space can twist, and it can ripple; so real that empty space itself helps shape everything in the world around us and forms the very fabric of the cosmos."

What Brian Greene is talking about here is that science is discovering that there is a "Mysterious Force" out in space, out in this nothingness, in this emptiness, and in the void, that is controlling our world. This force is more powerful than we can imagine. Our world, our galaxy, our universe is mostly empty space, and it is this "space" that dictates what happens here.

According to Brian, it seems that we actually live in an illusionary world, a sort of a matrix. The illusionary aspects are really driven home in this next quote from Brian Greene,

"In fact, if you removed all the space inside all the atoms making up the stone, glass and steel of the Empire State building, you would be left with a little lump, about the size of a grain of rice but weighing hundreds of millions of pounds. The rest is only empty space."

So maybe this is the meaning of nothingness in Zen, the knowing that all we see, feel and touch is nothing more than an illusion. There must be a way to attain freedom from this illusion and get out of the "stuff," and the "matrix," and see the true reality, the true reality that cannot be seen while still living in and under this illusion.

Science is telling us now that it is what we don't see or know that is the real factor in determining our fates as a species. Could it be that different from Eastern Thought? Within this mysterious emptiness, nothingness could be a whole another world where duality does not exist and the truth lives. There is something powerful out there and Zen knows what it is.

Enlightenment is like this, it is not in attaining truths, it is about removing the lies. The lies that have manifested in false beliefs. Once all the lies have been removed, there is nothing but space, complete emptiness, complete nothingness, that is where the real truth resides.

By removing choices, judgments, and separateness, by not trying to put meaning to everything, but to just reflect life, to become like the cloud, to search for nothing knowing that there is nothing to find, maybe this is the way to break free from the grain of rice and see the reality that the illusion is hiding from us. It is the clinging to false beliefs that has trapped us in this matrix. This is the purpose of Zen, to remove yourself from it and return to your true nature. To return to your true nature in this world, learn to use your mind and yet be free from any attachment. The true nature is unborn therefore undying, it neither moves or stays, it is already complete, and all that is needed is already here. Learn this principle.

An example of this is illustrated in this little story about when Hui Neng, the sixth and last patriarch of Chan, lay dying. One of the students there with him by his bedside asked, "Master, where are you going?" This question must be in reference as to where Hui Neng's soul would go upon death. Hui Neng replied, " What a foolish question? Where can one go? There is nowhere to go. One is always here, now."

What Hui Neng is saying that you are always here. There is no then or here then there. There is only now. That what has gone is gone and you can no more go to yesterday than you can go to tomorrow because you can only be here now. When tomorrow does come, then it is here now, it is always here now. There is no way you can be anywhere else. So therefore there isn't any place to go to and nobody to go anywhere. You are all with everything already, there is no fear of death, no dread nor no nirvana to achieve. Only now. There is nothing to be done, nothing to cling to, only just be. When a world comes to an end, another begins. Just like there was a yesterday, there will be a tomorrow, but till then there is only now so be here in this now, the yesterdays and tomorrows will take care of themselves in their own accord.

So live life and be aware of all that surrounds you. Learn to listen to the sound of the running water of a stream, or the sounds of the songbirds, become silent and quiet and learn to listen with your soul. Close your eyes and imagine that you are that waterfall or the songbird, feel the breeze as it blows through the tress and across the grass. Learn to listen to the connectiveness of it all. Learn to hear what isn't being said, learn to hear with your soul and true self. In the silence and quietness, you'll rediscover your Buddha-nature, your true authentic self, and experience what Seng-Ts'an is conveying in the Hsin Hsin Ming. Use the Hsin Hsin Ming as a guide to enlightenment.

"A true life has no need to raise waves when the wind is not blowing."

In seeking, you'll never find it. The very act of seeking creates separation. As long as separation exists, attainment cannot be had. Cease to seek and separation vanishes. Cease to seek to become whole.

32

Here is another view point on truth, and truth in the laws of nature from someone in the field of science. This is in order to show how completely different minds have at their core the same thoughts on truth, here is a quote from the renowned French mathematician Henri Poincare,

"The scientist does not study Nature because it is useful; he studies it because he delights in it, and he delights in it because it is beautiful. If Nature were not beautiful, it would not be worth knowing, and if Nature were not worth knowing, life would not be worth living."

Even through the perceived cold-hearted view of physics and mathematics, there is a lustrous desire to know the truth and the laws of nature, for they know that within this beauty is a truth, the truth that they are searching for.

This is the greatness of the Hsin Hsin Ming. The Hsin Hsin Ming contains within itself a central message that is universal and is capable of transcending all faiths, all religions, and all dogmas.

The second gate to enlightenment is through the "Entrance of Practice." There are four steps or increments that make up the principles to this entrance. The first step is the practice of accepting all sufferings with equanimity. to accept suffering as the results of past transgressions. And to do this without complaint or hatred. Knowing that this is nothing more than the fruits of seeds planted in the past. In plain English, to take what you got coming. To take it without letting it control your anger or to become enraged over it. Take it because you created it, it is yours and you own it. So deal with it.

The second step is the practice of accepting your circumstances, to know what is in your control and what isn't. That whatever may be, you'll embrace it equally. To know that no matter how great it may seem, or how horrible it can be, it is all transitory, all an illusion. Whatever role you are to play in this drama called life, play your role to the best of your ability. Accept your role, whether the character is to be a beggar or an Emperor, for this is your role to play.

The third step is to learn how to diminish your desires. In learning how to diminish your desires, you'll realize that suffering is brought about and rooted in desire. Therefore, eliminate desire and you eliminate suffering. Suffering is the result of clinging on to something. Suffering is caused by attachments. Do no attach yourself to anything that will bring pain upon its removal.

The forth step is to practice in accordance with the Dharma and to expel all thoughts that are wrong, hurtful, and of a lesser mind. In a pure mind there is no evil. In a lesser mind there is conflict and confusion. Like meets like in the lesser mind. When someone of a lesser mind is offended or hurt, they seek out to repay the offender with like minded justice. It is important to practice a pure mind and give compassion and forgiveness to those who cross you. For whatever you cast out to the world, you will reap in return.

With these four steps, it is possible for the true nature to be attained. The true nature here referring to the Buddha Nature.

What is remarkable about these steps is how much they resemble the precepts of Enchiridion by Epictetus, the Greek philosopher. In the Enchiridion, we clearly see the same lessons being taught. This is just another testament to the universal nature of the Tao and it can be found throughout all societies in all ages of man.

To show the universal nature of Zen, that everything you need is within you. Here is a quote from Plotinus, a third century Greek philosopher,

*"Withdraw into yourself and look. And if you don't find yourself beautiful yet, act as does the creator of a statue that is to be made beautiful: he cuts away here, he smoothes there, he makes this line lighter, this other purer, until a lovely face has grown from his work. So do you also: cut away all that is excessive, straighten all that is crooked, bring light to all that is overcast, labor to make all one glow or beauty and never cease to chiseling your statue, until there shall shine out on you from it the godlike splendor of virtue, until you see the prefect goodness surely established in the stainless shrine"*

You already have everything you need, it's time to wake up and flip the switch.

# ABOUT THE AUTHOR

Dennis M Waller is recognized as an expert on spiritual experience, self-discovery, and exploring the human consciousness. As writer, speaker and philosopher, his teachings invoke an introspective view on how to discover one's true authentic self through a higher sense of consciousness and awareness. He is best known for his work in the field of Indigos, people who possess unusual or supernatural abilities. His other fields of expertise include comparative religion, the law of attraction, and interpreting Eastern thought's relevancy to science and quantum physics. He is in demand as a guest speaker on radio programs, a lecturer at churches and life enrichment groups, and conducts workshops for Indigos.